FRAMEWORK

This Journal Belongs To:

____

____

____

____

What is the FrameWork Journal

A daily routine is important for a successful day, week, month, year and future.

Sometimes we don't know where to start. We are told to start our day with gratitude and end it with gratitude, but what do we do in between?

FrameWork helps you "frame" your day so you can effectively stay on target throughout the day. You can only go so far without a plan. This work helps you strategically map your way through your day.

This work also helps you identify and acknowledge those things that distract us throughout the day and assist you in moving pass them so that you can continue with what you have framed your day to be. We get hit with triggers and it completely sets our day off path and because we don't have any FrameWork for the day, we stay in that place of anger, sadness, depression, etc. and have no way of getting out of it.

Each part of FrameWork helps you plan each part of your day and recognize the distractions/triggers within your day and in return you attract the things that you most desire and are able to move through

your distractions by only focusing on the positive aspects of your life.

Welcome to “FrameWork”!

How To Use Your FrameWork Journal

Before You Begin, Account For Where Your Energy Is Going

-EVERYTHING IS ENERGY! With this being said, every thought that you have, everything that is weighing on you is energy. Account for this energy so that you can control it. Knowing what energy you have out will help you frame your day so that you are not focusing on 100 things at one time. If you have 100 pieces of energy out there, you are only putting 1% of your energy in that area and there will be no solutions in that area.

Step 1: Start Your Day With Gratitude

-List 10 things that you are grateful for. Doing this will start your day with a positive view of life. When you recognize the good, That's all that will come to you. Start your sentence off with something like, "I am so grateful for..." or something like "God, I thank you for...".

Step 2: What do I like about myself?

-Your view of yourself is damaging your view of the world and therefore only attracting how you feel

about yourself. Start loving yourself by pointing out one things a day that you LOVE about yourself. Not like, not feel so-so about, but LOVE about yourself. Doesn't matter what it is. Compliment and love on yourself and show yourself some gratitude.

Step 3: How do I want to feel at the end of the day?

-Tell yourself how you want to feel at the end of the day. This will help you direct your emotional focus for the day. Use this as a emotional focal point throughout the day to keep you on the path to a great day. No matter what happens throughout the day, remember what you told yourself about how your day was going to end. Do not feel discouraged. With all things, it takes practice. Use this to keep your emotions in check and it will also help you keep your thoughts together and only focused on the positive end goal.

Step 4: What do I want to have accomplished at the end of the day? How will I feel once I complete this task?

-Stop putting so much on yourself. Think of the one thing that you want to accomplish today. No matter what, focus on completing this one goal. Be specific and not general. For example, don't say, "I want to finish everything on my To-Do list."

Make it specific. "I am going to complete all tasks related to ____________."

Step 5: How will I use what comes to me today?

-Getting hit by things is naturally a part of life. It's called the Law of Opposites. Once you make a decision, the opposite is automatically created. You go left, and right automatically appears. That's the law. This step helps you channel the opposite for your good and not fall into what you see but what you believe. This will help you see the good in the opposite. THIS IS KEY IN ORDER TO REACH STEP 3 and will add to Step 2.

Step 6: How was your day?

-Just that. How was your day? When you do this part, only focus on the positive things about your day This step helps you to count your victories, helps you to see the positive in your day instead of focusing on what went wrong.

Step 7: How do you feel about your day?

-Now time for the big one. How do you feel about your day? Do you feel like you said you would? If not, why? Then ask yourself at what point did I allow myself to get off focused from my emotional goal for the day? This will help you see how one decision shifted your focus and help you to respond rather than react the next time it comes up or anything like it comes up.

Step 8: End with gratitude.

-End your day with gratitude. List 10 things that you are grateful for that happened during the day. This helps you end your day with happiness and gratitude and help you sleep well so that you can start the next day refreshed.

I Am Connected!!!

Where Is Your Energy Going:

Day:___________________

10 Things I am Grateful For:

What I like about myself?

How do I want to feel at the end of the day?

What do I want to have accomplished at the end of the day?
How will I feel once I complete this tasks?

How will I feel once I complete this tasks?

How will I use what comes to me today?

How was your day?

How do you feel about your day?

10 Things About The Day that you are grateful for.

***Day:*____________________**

10 Things I am Grateful For:

What I like about myself?

How do I want to feel at the end of the day?

What do I want to have accomplished at the end of the day?

How will I feel once I complete this tasks?

How will I feel once I complete this tasks?

How will I use what comes to me today?

How was your day?

How do you feel about your day?

10 Things About The Day that you are grateful for.

***Day:*__________________**

10 Things I am Grateful For:

What I like about myself?

How do I want to feel at the end of the day?

What do I want to have accomplished at the end of the day?
How will I feel once I complete this tasks?

How will I feel once I complete this tasks?

How will I use what comes to me today?

How was your day?

How do you feel about your day?

10 Things About The Day that you are grateful for.

Day:___________________

10 Things I am Grateful For:

What I like about myself?

How do I want to feel at the end of the day?

What do I want to have accomplished at the end of the day?
How will I feel once I complete this tasks?

How will I feel once I complete this tasks?

How will I use what comes to me today?

How was your day?

How do you feel about your day?

10 Things About The Day that you are grateful for.

Day:___________________

10 Things I am Grateful For:

What I like about myself?

How do I want to feel at the end of the day?

What do I want to have accomplished at the end of the day?
How will I feel once I complete this tasks?

How will I feel once I complete this tasks?

How will I use what comes to me today?

How was your day?

How do you feel about your day?

10 Things About The Day that you are grateful for.

Day:___________________

10 Things I am Grateful For:

What I like about myself?

How do I want to feel at the end of the day?

What do I want to have accomplished at the end of the day?
How will I feel once I complete this tasks?

How will I feel once I complete this tasks?

How will I use what comes to me today?

How was your day?

How do you feel about your day?

10 Things About The Day that you are grateful for.

Day:______________________

10 Things I am Grateful For:

What I like about myself?

How do I want to feel at the end of the day?

What do I want to have accomplished at the end of the day?
How will I feel once I complete this tasks?

How will I feel once I complete this tasks?

How will I use what comes to me today?

How was your day?

How do you feel about your day?

10 Things About The Day that you are grateful for.

Day:___________________

10 Things I am Grateful For:

What I like about myself?

How do I want to feel at the end of the day?

What do I want to have accomplished at the end of the day?
How will I feel once I complete this tasks?

How will I feel once I complete this tasks?

How will I use what comes to me today?

How was your day?

How do you feel about your day?

10 Things About The Day that you are grateful for.

Day:___________________

10 Things I am Grateful For:

What I like about myself?

How do I want to feel at the end of the day?

What do I want to have accomplished at the end of the day?
How will I feel once I complete this tasks?

How will I feel once I complete this tasks?

How will I use what comes to me today?

How was your day?

How do you feel about your day?

10 Things About The Day that you are grateful for.

***Day:*____________________**

10 Things I am Grateful For:

What I like about myself?

How do I want to feel at the end of the day?

What do I want to have accomplished at the end of the day?

How will I feel once I complete this tasks?

How will I feel once I complete this tasks?

How will I use what comes to me today?

How was your day?

How do you feel about your day?

10 Things About The Day that you are grateful for.

***Day:*____________________**

10 Things I am Grateful For:

What I like about myself?

How do I want to feel at the end of the day?

What do I want to have accomplished at the end of the day?
How will I feel once I complete this tasks?

How will I feel once I complete this tasks?

How will I use what comes to me today?

How was your day?

How do you feel about your day?

10 Things About The Day that you are grateful for.

Day:___________________

10 Things I am Grateful For:

What I like about myself?

How do I want to feel at the end of the day?

What do I want to have accomplished at the end of the day?
How will I feel once I complete this tasks?

How will I feel once I complete this tasks?

How will I use what comes to me today?

How was your day?

How do you feel about your day?

10 Things About The Day that you are grateful for.

***Day:*____________________**

10 Things I am Grateful For:

What I like about myself?

How do I want to feel at the end of the day?

What do I want to have accomplished at the end of the day?
How will I feel once I complete this tasks?

How will I feel once I complete this tasks?

How will I use what comes to me today?

How was your day?

How do you feel about your day?

10 Things About The Day that you are grateful for.

Day:___________________

10 Things I am Grateful For:

What I like about myself?

How do I want to feel at the end of the day?

What do I want to have accomplished at the end of the day?
How will I feel once I complete this tasks?

How will I feel once I complete this tasks?

How will I use what comes to me today?

How was your day?

How do you feel about your day?

10 Things About The Day that you are grateful for.

Day:___________________

10 Things I am Grateful For:

What I like about myself?

How do I want to feel at the end of the day?

What do I want to have accomplished at the end of the day?
How will I feel once I complete this tasks?

How will I feel once I complete this tasks?

How will I use what comes to me today?

How was your day?

How do you feel about your day?

10 Things About The Day that you are grateful for.

Day:___________________

10 Things I am Grateful For:

What I like about myself?

How do I want to feel at the end of the day?

What do I want to have accomplished at the end of the day?
How will I feel once I complete this tasks?

How will I feel once I complete this tasks?

How will I use what comes to me today?

How was your day?

How do you feel about your day?

10 Things About The Day that you are grateful for.

***Day:*____________________**

10 Things I am Grateful For:

What I like about myself?

How do I want to feel at the end of the day?

What do I want to have accomplished at the end of the day?
How will I feel once I complete this tasks?

How will I feel once I complete this tasks?

How will I use what comes to me today?

How was your day?

How do you feel about your day?

10 Things About The Day that you are grateful for.

***Day:*____________________**

10 Things I am Grateful For:

What I like about myself?

How do I want to feel at the end of the day?

What do I want to have accomplished at the end of the day?
How will I feel once I complete this tasks?

How will I feel once I complete this tasks?

How will I use what comes to me today?

How was your day?

How do you feel about your day?

10 Things About The Day that you are grateful for.

Day:_____________________

10 Things I am Grateful For:

What I like about myself?

How do I want to feel at the end of the day?

What do I want to have accomplished at the end of the day?
How will I feel once I complete this tasks?

How will I feel once I complete this tasks?

How will I use what comes to me today?

How was your day?

How do you feel about your day?

10 Things About The Day that you are grateful for.

***Day:*______________________**

10 Things I am Grateful For:

What I like about myself?

How do I want to feel at the end of the day?

What do I want to have accomplished at the end of the day?
How will I feel once I complete this tasks?

How will I feel once I complete this tasks?

How will I use what comes to me today?

How was your day?

How do you feel about your day?

10 Things About The Day that you are grateful for.

Day:___________________

10 Things I am Grateful For:

What I like about myself?

How do I want to feel at the end of the day?

What do I want to have accomplished at the end of the day?
How will I feel once I complete this tasks?

How will I feel once I complete this tasks?

How will I use what comes to me today?

How was your day?

How do you feel about your day?

10 Things About The Day that you are grateful for.

Day:______________________

10 Things I am Grateful For:

What I like about myself?

How do I want to feel at the end of the day?

What do I want to have accomplished at the end of the day?
How will I feel once I complete this tasks?

How will I feel once I complete this tasks?

How will I use what comes to me today?

How was your day?

How do you feel about your day?

10 Things About The Day that you are grateful for.

Day:___________________

10 Things I am Grateful For:

What I like about myself?

How do I want to feel at the end of the day?

What do I want to have accomplished at the end of the day?
How will I feel once I complete this tasks?

How will I feel once I complete this tasks?

How will I use what comes to me today?

How was your day?

How do you feel about your day?

10 Things About The Day that you are grateful for.

***Day:*____________________**

10 Things I am Grateful For:

What I like about myself?

How do I want to feel at the end of the day?

What do I want to have accomplished at the end of the day?
How will I feel once I complete this tasks?

How will I feel once I complete this tasks?

How will I use what comes to me today?

How was your day?

How do you feel about your day?

10 Things About The Day that you are grateful for.

Day:___________________

10 Things I am Grateful For:

What I like about myself?

How do I want to feel at the end of the day?

What do I want to have accomplished at the end of the day?
How will I feel once I complete this tasks?

How will I feel once I complete this tasks?

How will I use what comes to me today?

How was your day?

How do you feel about your day?

10 Things About The Day that you are grateful for.

***Day:*____________________**

10 Things I am Grateful For:

What I like about myself?

How do I want to feel at the end of the day?

What do I want to have accomplished at the end of the day?
How will I feel once I complete this tasks?

How will I feel once I complete this tasks?

How will I use what comes to me today?

How was your day?

How do you feel about your day?

10 Things About The Day that you are grateful for.

Day:______________________

10 Things I am Grateful For:

What I like about myself?

How do I want to feel at the end of the day?

What do I want to have accomplished at the end of the day?
How will I feel once I complete this tasks?

How will I feel once I complete this tasks?

How will I use what comes to me today?

How was your day?

How do you feel about your day?

10 Things About The Day that you are grateful for.

Day: ____________________

10 Things I am Grateful For:

What I like about myself?

How do I want to feel at the end of the day?

What do I want to have accomplished at the end of the day?
How will I feel once I complete this tasks?

How will I feel once I complete this tasks?

How will I use what comes to me today?

How was your day?

How do you feel about your day?

10 Things About The Day that you are grateful for.

***Day:*__________________**

10 Things I am Grateful For:

What I like about myself?

How do I want to feel at the end of the day?

What do I want to have accomplished at the end of the day?
How will I feel once I complete this tasks?

How will I feel once I complete this tasks?

How will I use what comes to me today?

How was your day?

How do you feel about your day?

10 Things About The Day that you are grateful for.

***Day:*____________________**

10 Things I am Grateful For:

What I like about myself?

How do I want to feel at the end of the day?

What do I want to have accomplished at the end of the day?
How will I feel once I complete this tasks?

How will I feel once I complete this tasks?

How will I use what comes to me today?

How was your day?

How do you feel about your day?

10 Things About The Day that you are grateful for.

Day:___________________

10 Things I am Grateful For:

What I like about myself?

How do I want to feel at the end of the day?

What do I want to have accomplished at the end of the day?
How will I feel once I complete this tasks?

How will I feel once I complete this tasks?

How will I use what comes to me today?

How was your day?

How do you feel about your day?

10 Things About The Day that you are grateful for.

"*I Am*" Affirmations for <u>You</u>

✧ I Am Allowing
✧ I Am Abundance
✧ I Am Freedom
✧ I Am Forgiveness
✧ I Am Beautiful
✧ I Am Love
✧ I Am Bold
✧ I Am Alive
✧ I Am Light
✧ I Am Grateful
✧ I Am Prosperity
✧ I Am A Student
✧ I Am Enough
✧ I Am Greatness and Achieve It Constantly
✧ I Am Worthy
✧ I Am Open To Receive
✧ I Am Successful
✧ I Am My Ancestor's Greatest Dreams
✧ I Am Free
✧ I Am Peace
✧ I Love You
✧ I Am Savage